MIX
Papier aus verantwortungsvollen Quellen
Paper from responsible sources
FSC® C105338
FSC
www.fsc.org

Emmeline Cambridge

Exploring the Effect of Imagery and Categorisation on Belief in Animal Mind

Anchor Academic
Publishing

Cambridge, Emmeline: Exploring the Effect of Imagery and Categorisation on Belief in
Animal Mind, Hamburg, Anchor Academic Publishing 2017

Buch-ISBN: 978-3-95489-411-6
PDF-eBook-ISBN: 978-3-95489-489-5
Druck/Herstellung: Anchor Academic Publishing, Hamburg, 2017

Bibliografische Information der Deutschen Nationalbibliothek:
Die Deutsche Nationalbibliothek verzeichnet diese Publikation in der Deutschen
Nationalbibliografie; detaillierte bibliografische Daten sind im Internet über
http://dnb.d-nb.de abrufbar.

Bibliographical Information of the German National Library:
The German National Library lists this publication in the German National Bibliography.
Detailed bibliographic data can be found at: http://dnb.d-nb.de

All rights reserved. This publication may not be reproduced, stored in a retrieval system
or transmitted, in any form or by any means, electronic, mechanical, photocopying,
recording or otherwise, without the prior permission of the publishers.

Das Werk einschließlich aller seiner Teile ist urheberrechtlich geschützt. Jede Verwertung
außerhalb der Grenzen des Urheberrechtsgesetzes ist ohne Zustimmung des Verlages
unzulässig und strafbar. Dies gilt insbesondere für Vervielfältigungen, Übersetzungen,
Mikroverfilmungen und die Einspeicherung und Bearbeitung in elektronischen Systemen.

Die Wiedergabe von Gebrauchsnamen, Handelsnamen, Warenbezeichnungen usw. in
diesem Werk berechtigt auch ohne besondere Kennzeichnung nicht zu der Annahme,
dass solche Namen im Sinne der Warenzeichen- und Markenschutz-Gesetzgebung als frei
zu betrachten wären und daher von jedermann benutzt werden dürften.

Die Informationen in diesem Werk wurden mit Sorgfalt erarbeitet. Dennoch können
Fehler nicht vollständig ausgeschlossen werden und die Diplomica Verlag GmbH, die
Autoren oder Übersetzer übernehmen keine juristische Verantwortung oder irgendeine
Haftung für evtl. verbliebene fehlerhafte Angaben und deren Folgen.

Alle Rechte vorbehalten

© Anchor Academic Publishing, Imprint der Diplomica Verlag GmbH
Hermannstal 119k, 22119 Hamburg
http://www.diplomica-verlag.de, Hamburg 2017
Printed in Germany

Table of Contents

Abstract 3
Categorisation 5
   Cognitive dissonance 5
   Cognitive dissonance and Belief in animal mind 7
   Attitudes towards animal use 10
   Imagery as a variable 12
   The present study 13
Method 14
   Design 14
   Participants 14
      Control condition 14
      Experimental condition 14
   Materials 15
      Demographic information 15
      Attitudes towards the treatment of animals scale 15
      Mental capacity scale 15
      Procedure 16
      Ethical considerations 16
Results 18
   Hypothesis one 18
   Hypothesis two 19
   Hypothesis three 20
   Hypothesis four 21
Discussion 22
   Category 22
   ATAS 24
   Presentation 24
References 27
Appendices 32

Abstract

Following the horse meat scandal of 2012 the concept of the meat paradox was created; engaging in the consumption of meat whilst simultaneously disliking hurting animals. The theory of cognitive dissonance suggests than farm animals are denied mind in order to relieve negative feelings associated with eating animals. The present study explores the hypotheses that animals will be attributed mind based on their category. The effect of the presentation of the animal (e.g. text/image) on animal mind is also tested, as well as association between mind attitudes toward animals. 69 participants recruited using the Hanover social research website and University of Worcester research scheme completed this study.

Participants completed a demographic questionnaire followed by the attitudes towards animals scale (ATAS) and an animal mental capacity rating task (in either the control (text) or experimental condition (image) conditions. The animals formed a number of categories, including food and companion animals. A mixed ANOVA revealed no significant interaction between the presentation of the animal (word/image) and BAM. Presentation was also found no have no significant effect on BAM, despite a consistently lower average of BAM in the word condition. A significant effect was however, found for animal category on BAM, with the largest differences lying between companion animals and the other categories (pest, food, cold). Furthermore, there was no significant association between attitudes towards animal and BAM.

In conclusion there is a clear and well supported relationship between animal category and belief animal, which has been demonstrated for not only food animals, but also for pest and cold blooded animals. Future research should further explore the relationship various categories of animals and BAM.

In 2013, UK citizens were forced to consider the origins of their products when perceptions towards meat were challenged following the exposure of the horse-meat scandal in Europe. Tests revealed foods advertised as beef burger products to contain both undeclared horse and pig DNA. These contaminated products, in some cases containing up to 100% horse-meat (Morris, 2014) were sold by numerous retailers, including Tesco, Aldi and Iceland (Food Safety Authority of Ireland, 2013).

Questions were roused regarding perceptions towards different meat sources as consumers held the perception that they were eating products derived from pigs (pork) and cows (beef) (Persaud, 2013). The same individuals however, were disgusted at the concept of consuming horse meat "In Ireland, it is not our culture to eat horsemeat and therefore, we do not expect to find it in a burger" (Food Safety Authority of Ireland, 2013). This raises the question of the difference between conventional food animals such as cows, and other animals such as horses.

Furthermore, the nature of meat consumption in general was also explored, questioning why humans appear to demonstrate natural empathy towards living things and yet consume a product that demands the killing and suffering of an animal. It argues that the consumption of meat, itself, is paradoxical in nature - humans appear to demonstrate a natural empathy towards animals and when witnessing their suffering causes a significant level of distress. This contradiction of behaviour and beliefs has been dubbed 'the meat paradox'.

There is an increasing amount of research surrounding attitudes towards meat and animals, perhaps reflecting a growing interest in the sources and quality of meat, as well as concern for animal welfare. A recent poll found that almost a third of respondents said the horsemeat scandal had "permanently impacted" the way they chose and bought food. (Morris, 2014)

This study aims to re-evaluate attitudes towards food animals in light of the recent focus in the media on farm-animal welfare and the sources of meat. By exploring the nature of the meat paradox and investigating the perceptions of food animals compared to other animals, this study builds upon previous research by introducing a new combination of variables and methodology. The extent to which animals are perceived to possess mental capacities, as the dependent variable will be measured and compared across two independent variables; type of presentation of animal (text/image) and animal category (e.g. food/companion).

Categorisation

In exploring the human relationship with animals, research has found that placing animals into categories can have a significant influence on how they are treated (Herzog, 2010), which is clearly supported by the difference in the legal rights of food animals compared to companion animals.

A recent study conducted by Bratanova, Loughnan, & Bastian (2011) aimed to investigate the role of categorisation on attitudes towards meat animals. Participants were presented with an animal that they had never encountered before (a tree kangaroo) and in one condition, were told the animal was considered food, and in the other condition (control) no mention of food or meat was made. It was found that participants in the food group attributed significantly less moral rights to the animal than those in the control condition. These findings suggest that simply being classed as a food animal results in being attributed fewer moral rights.

The bias demonstrated in this study has been named speciesism, which has been the focus of recent research at University of Melbourne. This term was first used during the 1970's to describe discrimination against nonhuman animals, although it is currently often extended to any of those not classed as belonging to a particular species. The new area of animal law recently introduced at the university sets out to address the issue of speciesism within a legal framework. The concept of speciesism is important in explaining the meat paradox as research suggests it is the animals' category that determines its individual treatment. A potential reason for this is cognitive dissonance.

Cognitive dissonance

Theories explaining the meat paradox focus highly on the concept of cognitive dissonance. Cognitive dissonance has been defined as an undesirable emotional state that arises from holding two conflicting beliefs (Harmon-Jones & Mills, 1999). This was first described by Festinger (1957) who proposed that this unpleasant state of discomfort arises when an individual holds two or more relevant elements of knowledge/cognitions that are inconsistent with other. In his theory of cognitive dissonance, Festinger (1957) stated that humans have an inner drive to hold attitudes/beliefs (cognitions) in harmony (or consistency). When these elements are not consistent, the state of dissonance is created leaving the individual with a limited number of options for reducing this unpleasant state.

When the theory of cognitive dissonance is applied to the meat paradox, the caring attitude towards animals and the desire for meat form the opposing cognitions. In order to reduce the resulting dissonance, Festinger described a number of mechanisms. Firstly, a cognitive method may be used by acquiring new information that outweighs the dissonance cognitions. For example, discovering new research that questions the validity of the relationship between smoking and cancer may reduce dissonance by causing doubt towards old information. Secondly, the importance of a cognition can be reduced. For example, placing focusing on the present day and 'living for the moment' in order to decrease the importance of the belief that smoking is likely to cause a premature death. Finally, the individual may change their attitude, belief or behaviour to be consistent with other cognitions.

When one of the dissonant elements is a behaviour, such as smoking or eating meat, the behaviour can ultimately be eliminated. However, this if often difficult for behaviours with conditioned responses (such as the reward of nicotine from smoking). In the case of meat, the behaviour could be eliminated by becoming a vegetarian, however Festinger (1957) argues that if confronted with two simultaneous opposing beliefs, it is likely the perception of the individual will change rather their belief or their behaviour.

This is supported by the original study that inspired the theory. Festinger (1957) followed a religious group that had predicted an apocalyptic event. The leader of the group, claimed that superior beings from another planet were communicating with her, saying her group would be saved from the cataclysm. Festinger aimed to examine how the group members would deal with the upcoming conflict in beliefs when the prediction failed to come true. On the date of the 'apocalypse' the group leader declared she had received a message stating God had saved them from the world of destruction, following which the group began recruitment with even more commitment than before.

According to Festinger's theory, the conflict experienced by the Seekers between reality and prophecy was resolved by increasing their numbers, stating "If more people can be persuaded that the system of belief is correct, then clearly, it must, after all, be correct" (Festinger, Riecken, & Schachter, 1956). This early research on cognitive dissonance has since been applied to a number of different research areas. In the 5 years however, the number of studies examining cognitive dissonance in the context of meat consumption have increased dramatically. A number of studies over recent years have been conducted by Loughnan and Bastian (Loughnan, Haslam, & Bastian, 2010) (Bratanova, Loughnan, & Bastian, 2011) (Bastian, 2012), providing the key current literature on the meat paradox.

When the theory of cognitive dissonance is applied to the meat paradox, the caring attitude towards animals and the desire for meat form the opposing beliefs. In this situation, it is the perception of the animals that change, rather than attitudes or behaviour. The key way in which perception is thought to change is through the denial of mind to food animals, also known as de-mentalisation (Kozak, Marsh, & Wegner, 2006).

Cognitive dissonance and Belief in animal mind
The attribution of mental capacities to animals, such as feelings of emotion and intellect, has now been defined as Belief in Animal Mind (BAM). Despite original uncertainty, there is now general agreement in the scientific community that non-human animals have the capacity for sentience. The Cambridge Declaration on Consciousness (Low, et al., 2012) is stated "Convergent evidence indicates that non-human animals have the neuroanatomical, neurochemical, and neurophysiological substrates of conscious states along with the capacity to exhibit intentional behaviours". Charles Darwin recognised sentience as "an essential feature of evolutionary fitness and believed it to be widespread in the animal world" (Darwin, 1871).

The significance of research supporting the possession of animal mind is supported by studies showing when people do not believe animals capable of thinking/feeling, they are more inclined to support animal use (Herzog & Galvin, 2007). It can be questioned however whether dementalisation has actually occurred. For example, it is unclear if animals used in research are denied mind in favor of academic knowledge, or whether they are perceived to possess little mind irrespective of the situation. In order to investigate this Loughnan and Bastian (2011) examined the attitudes of vegetarians and omnivores towards the mental capacities of meat animals upon being reminded that they would be killed. It was found that vegetarians showed no change in their attribution of mental states following the reminder. However, by contrast, when the omnivores were reminded they attributed fewer mental states. The finding that vegetarians showed no change is in line with previous research that has found individuals with strong views are less susceptible to changes in attitude (Chaiken & Baldwin, 1981).

A series of further studies conducted by Bastian and colleagues aimed to investigate the attribution of sentience in farm animals (Bastian, 2012). This research set out to prove that consumers of meat undergo a lengthy cognitive process in order to overcome inconsistencies between their beliefs (i.e. concern for animal welfare) and behaviours (meat consumption). The three separate studies investigated an aspect of this process.

In study one, it was hypothesised that when people want to reduce the conflict between moral concern for animals and eating meat, they will deny mind to the animal being consumed. Participants were first year Psychology university students, the majority of whom were female. Participants were required to rate 32 animals using a 7-point scale, based on the degree to which they are believed to possess ten mental capacities. The animals chosen to be included in this study were based on previous research (Grey, Grey, & Wegner, 2007); (Laham, 2009); (Morewedge, C., Preston, & Wegner, 2007). This use of previously used materials increases the internal validity of this study. Participants were also required to indicate the edibility or each animal and how bad they would feel for consuming it.

This research found perceived level of mind to be negatively associated with an animal's edibility and positively associated with both negative feelings involved with its consumption and moral opposition to eating the animal. These findings confirmed the experimental hypothesis showing that animals that are considered appropriate for consumption are attribution less mind than those considered inappropriate; a process known as dementalisation. This supports the theory that food animals may be ascribed diminished mental capacities in order to avoid feelings of guilt regarding their consumption. Although these findings demonstrate that food animals are attributed fewer mental capacities than other animals, it could be argued that this is not necessarily as mechanism for reducing dissonance. In the present study it is predicted that participants will attribute fewer mental capacities to food animals than companion animals (hypothesis 1).

In order to extend the findings of the first study, Bastian conducted a follow up study in which he aimed to control feelings of dissonance in order to demonstrate the denial of mind as a mechanism for reducing dissonance. According to Festinger's theory, when participants are reminded of the suffering of food animals, they would be more inclined to deny the animals mind, thus reducing negative state and facilitating their meat-eating behaviour.

Participants completed a questionnaire (one of two versions) that required them to look at an image (sheep/cow), followed by a description of the animal (either referencing its purpose as food or not). An independent samples t test indicated that when reminded an animal would be used for food, participants would ascribe them fewer mental capacities, compared to when no reminders were provided. These findings suggest that the reminders prompted a state of cognitive dissonance, causing the alteration of perception via dementalisation, thus reducing dissonance.

Based upon these findings the aim of study three was to test the role of behavioural commitment in motivating dissonance. It was predicted that similar to study two, participants whom were expecting to eat meat in the immediate future will be more motivated to reduce dissonance by denying the animal mind, than participants expecting to eat fruit (control condition).

As in study one participants completed the cow/sheep rating task (Time 1, T1). Participants were then told they would be sampling either apples (low dissonance condition) or beef/lamb (high dissonance condition). Both conditions then required participants to write an essay on the origins of beef/lamb, during which they were presented with their respective samples. Participants were again given the cow/sheep rating task (Time 2, T2).

Mind ratings at T1 and T2 across the two conditions were compared using a mixed ANOVA. A main effect of time was found, with animals denied more mental capacities at T2 than T1. Furthermore, there was also a significant interaction between time and condition. While there was no difference between T1 and T2 for the fruit condition, a significant reduction from T1 to T2 was found for the meat condition. Although there were no significant differences between conditions at T1, at T2 mind ratings were significantly lower in the meat condition than in the fruit condition. These findings support the theory of cognitive dissonance by showing that engaging in meat consumption appears to alter levels of belief in animal mind (BAM).

As the research of Bastian is so significant in this area of research, the studies must be critically analysed to determine the validity of the findings. Upon initial examination of the validity of the research conducted by Bastian, the external validity appears to be lacking. The population validity is particularly weak, with all participants in the first study being first year psychology students, as well as participants in the third study being offered the incentive of $10 or course credit for taking part in the research. Males are also under-represented in this research with study 3 using an exclusively female sample. Furthermore, all three studies were conducted in a laboratory space in a university setting, which limits the ecological validity of the findings.

The research however has strong internal validity, accounting for the possible demand characteristics risked by using psychology students. By making no mention of meat in recruitment materials, participants were led to believe they were taking part in a study of 'perceiving animals' mental states. This means that the confounding effect of demand characteristics is limited.

While the focus has been on the dissonance experienced by meat consumers, little attention has been given to other consumer groups (i.e. vegans and vegetarians), with non-meat eaters even being excluded from the studies.

Attitudes towards animal use

The research conducted by Bastian et al established that denying mind to animals can help reduce cognitive dissonance in the context of meat. Investigating the belief in animal mind from a different perspective comes a study conducted by (Knight, Vrij, Cherryman, & Nunkoosing, 2004), that investigates the relationship between BAM and attitudes towards animal use. This research is based on the theory that a belief in animal mind is a predictor of attitudes towards animal use, with specific individual characteristics that are thought to influence the perception of animal minds.

Knight et al (2004) investigated the hypotheses that participants with higher levels of BAM would be less supportive of animal use than those with lower levels of BAM. It was also predicted that males, older participants and meat-eaters (compared to vegetarians) to be more supportive of animal use.

The research found that BAM, gender and eating meat were significantly related to attitudes towards animal use. While gender and eating meat had a minimal effect, BAM was demonstrated as the most powerful predictor of attitudes towards animals, despite no causal relationship being able to be established. These findings may support the theory of the denial of mind as it demonstrates the differences in attitudes towards animals with high and low mental capacities. It is predicted that in the present study, participants who display more positive attitudes towards animals will attribute greater levels of mental capacity (demonstrate higher levels of BAM), than those with more negative attitudes towards animal (hypothesis 2).

On the other hand, little support was found for the effect of other variables on attitudes towards animals. Upon examination of the relationship between attitudes and age, the only significant relationship was found for the animal management category; younger participants were significantly less supportive than older participants. Knight et al (2004) suggests that this may be due to the particular statements in this category, (all of which describe a wild animal in their natural environment), in that young people may have different views towards wild animals compared to food or companion animals. It could therefore be argued that the relationship between age and attitudes towards animal use is only applicable in the case of wild animals.

The effect of numerous variables was not only investigated for its relationship with attitudes towards animals, but also with the belief in animal mind. It was found that age was the only predictor of BAM, with older participants displaying higher level of BAM than younger participants. The significance of these findings is due to the observed relationship between attitudes towards animals and belief in animal mind. In order to gain a more in depth understanding of this relationship, the influence of other variables (such as age) should be investigated. This is because it could be argued that the relationship may be due, at least in part, to the influence of other variables.

A number of various instruments have designed to measures attitudes towards animals. Research conducted by (Henry, 2004) aimed to examine the relationship between a history of observing or engaging in acts of animal cruelty and 'attitudes of sensitivity' towards the maltreatment of nonhuman animals, as well as a number of variables such as previous pet ownership. Attitudes of sensitivity were measured using the Attitudes toward the Treatment of animals Scale. Developed by Henry (2004), the 26-item scale required participants to indicate the extent to which they would be bothered by thinking about a particular type of treatment of an animal.

The findings of the study supported the main body of research revealing a significant main effect for gender on the ATAS, with women exhibiting greater concern regarding the treatment of animals than men. Gender also had a moderating effect on the relationship between the observation of animal cruelty and attitudes towards the treatment of animals. It was found that women who observed animal cruelty presented greater sensitivity regarding the treatment of animals, while men who observed animal cruelty exhibited lower sensitivity, scoring lower on the ATAS. As suggested by the author, the moderating effect of gender on the relationship between observation of animal cruelty and ATAS was an unexpected finding and should be explored in future research (Henry, 2004). These findings however, are limited as participants comprised solely of psychology students whose research participation was a requirement of the course, although both genders are well represented in the sample, with 92 (54.4%) female and 77 (45.6%) male participants.

As research has demonstrated the influence of numerous variables on attitudes towards animals and BAM, it is logical to question if the same variables will effects the level of bias displayed towards food and companion animals. Furthermore, more research is needed that may control or manipulate BAM or attitudes towards animals in order to establish a causal relationship.

Imagery as a variable
Supporters of the animal rights movement have already recognised the power of language in influencing attitudes towards animals and in response tries to change current language in support of animal rights (Stibbe, 2001). Examples of the lexical representations of animals used in the meat industry include product labelling using

terms "beef" instead of cow, or "pork" instead on pig. By using this terminology the animal is represented as a meat resource for humans, concealing the connection between the product and the killing of a live, sentient being (Singer, 1990; Stibbe, 2001).

More recently research has been conducted on the influence of different types of imagery on attitudes towards animal rights. An experiment conducted by Monterio (2012) required participants to complete a questionnaire that included a number of 'fake' advertisements (acting as a control) and an animal rights advertisement. The images of the farmed animals were classed as low, moderate and high in graphic detail. The Wuensch Animal Rights Scale was used to measure the effect of the images on attitudes towards animal rights (Wuensch, Jenkins, & Poteat, 2002).

It was found that the low detail image was the most effective at increasing scores on the animal rights scale (where higher scores equal stronger attitudes towards animal rights). This was followed by the moderate detail image, and the high detail image being the least effective. However, this effect was not statistically significant.

This study suggests that different types of imagery may influence the way people perceive animals. In the present study it is predicted that participants in the image condition will attribute lower levels of BAM than those in the word condition. Furthermore, a significant interaction is predicted between presentation of the animal (i.e. image, word) and animal category on BAM.

The present study
The current study expands on the current literature exploring the various factors effecting the attribution of mind in animals. Research has already demonstrated the relationship between attitudes towards animals and BAM but research has yet to explore this relationship in the context of the meat paradox. By focusing on the comparison of food animals with other categories, the present study explores the effect of imagery and categorisation on BAM, alongside testing for a signification association between attitudes towards animals and BAM.

Method

Design

This research incorporates a quantitative, mixed factorial design. Independent measures were used for the presentation of the animal variable (text/image) with participants taking part in either the control (text) or experimental (image) condition. Repeated measures, on the other hand were used for the type of animal (food; companion; wild; pest) with participants in both conditions being exposed to every category.

Participants

A total number of 94 individuals participated in this research, 69 of whom completed all conditions, while 25 partially completed the study by withdrawing following the second questionnaire (the ATAS). This gave a completion rate of 73%. 37 participants (54%) were assigned to the control condition and 32 to the experimental condition (46%).

Control condition

30 (81%) participants were women, and 7 (19%) participants were men. The mean age was 30 years ($SD = 15.41$), with a range of 1947 to 1999 years. 26 participants identified themselves as White (70%), 2 Hispanic/Latino; 5%, 2 Asian/Pacific Islander (5%), 2 Black/African American (5%), 2 mixed ethnicity (5%) and 2 preferred not to answer (5%). 1 participant did not answer (3%).

Participants were recruited using various methods. 35 (95%) participants were recruited via the Hanover research website (a research website that allows members of the public to participate in online research by following the link to the current study) and 2 (5%) using a personal Facebook page.

Experimental condition

29 (91%) participants were women, and 3 (9%) were men. The mean age was 37 years ($SD = 18.97$), with a range of 1941 to 1991 years. 25 participants identified themselves as White (86%), 1 Hispanic/Latino (3%), 3 Asian/Pacific Islander (9%), 1 mixed ethnicity (3%), 1 preferred not to answer (3%) and 1 participant did not answer (3%).

15 (47%) participants were recruited via the Hanover research; 10 (31%) using the University of Worcester RPT credit scheme (exclusively undergraduate psychology students), 6 (19%) using a personal Facebook page, and 1 (3%) using call for participants.

It should be noted that undergraduate psychology students were offered 30 RPT credits (corresponding to the 30 minute time requirement) for participating in this research, while other participant groups were offered no incentive.

Materials

Demographic information

Questionnaire designed to collect demographic and dietary information (See appendix 1A). The main variables with this section include age and ethnicity.

Attitudes towards the treatment of animals scale (Henry, 2004)

A 26-item attitude scale developed by (B) to assess sensitivity towards the maltreatment of animals. Participants were asked to indicate the extent to which they would be bothered by thinking about a particular type of treatment of an animal. Each item is phrased "How much would it bother you to think about..." For example, "How much would it bother you to think about someone intentionally killing a domestic stock animal other than for food or to help the animal because the animal was hurt, old, or sick?" (The full scale can be found in the Appendix 2B).

Participants indicated their answers using a 5-point scale ranging from 5, 'A lot' to 1, 'None at all'. Total scores range from 25 – 125, with higher scores reflecting greater discomfort with the maltreatment of animal animals. Previous research has found good internal consistency within their sample (alpha = 0.93).

Mental capacity scale

A survey was constructed and used to measure the level of mental capacities attributed to a range of difference animals (or belief in animal mind). These capacities were adapted from previous work on mind perception (Gray et al, 2007) and include the five highest loading experience-related capacities (hunger, fear, pleasure, pain and rage) and agency-related capacities (self-control, morality, memory, emotion, cognition, planning).

Participants were required to indicate on a 7-point Likert scale, the extent to which a range of animals possess different mental capacities. The animals included Food animals (cow, pig, sheep, chicken, goose, lamb), companion animals (dog, cat, horse, parrot, hamster, rabbit), wild mammals (lion, elephant, panda bear, dolphin, buffalo, gorilla), wild reptiles / amphibians (crocodile, frog, snake, komodo dragon, turtle, lizard) and pest animals (rat, fox, seagull, slug, badger, pigeon). In the control condition the animals were represented by text, and in the experimental condition by an image (see appendix 3C).

Procedure

This study was conducted online using SurveyMonkey. All participants participated in all 3 sections of the research, being randomly assigned to one of two presentation conditions for the third section. Participants were presented with an information sheet and consent form which required participants to accept the conditions of the research and click 'proceed' before being taken to the first questionnaire.

Participants provided basic demographic information by selecting their response from the lists displayed. Following this section, participants were taken to the Attitudes Towards Animals scale, where they were instructed to select one response for each question, ranging on a scale between 1 (not at all) and 5 (a lot) for a total of 26 items. Upon completion of the ATAS participants were presented with the mental capacity survey, either with images or text depending upon the link given to the participant, which is randomly assigned. Participants were asked to indicate on a 7-point Likert scale, the extent to which they believed a range of animals to possess different mental capacities.

Ethical considerations

Although there are no immediate ethical concerns for this research, standard safeguards have been incorporated into the design in consideration of BPS ethical guidelines. This includes no requirement of participants to disclose any identifying information such as name or address, as well as access the raw data being held only by those with access to the University of Worcester SurveyMonkey account. To increase confidentiality this data was regularly downloaded to a secure password protection laptop and deleted from the online account. Once the raw data collected from participants has been fully analysed it will be erased in all locations (including back-ups files).

The participants were also provided with an information sheet and consent form (Appendix 4D) that they were required to read and sign before beginning the research, in order to gain informed consent. The Ethics Checklist, completed Approval Form and Ethical approval code for this research can be found in appendix 5E.

Results

There were no outliers in the data, as assessed by inspection of boxplots for values greater than 1.5 box-lengths from the edge of the box.

BAM was normally distributed for both conditions across all categories ($p > .05$), with the exception of companion and mammals in the word condition ($p < .05$), as assessed by Shapiro-Wilk's test. There was homogeneity of variance ($p > .05$) for all categories but mammals, as assessed by Levene's test of homogeneity of variance. A number of transformations were used in an attempt to correct for unequal variances, however these were not successful. Mammals were therefore removed from further analysis.

There was homogeneity of covariances, as assessed by Box's test of equality of covariance matrices ($p = .022$). Following a mixed ANOVA, the data was checked for the assumption of sphericity, which was violated ($p < .05$). As the epsilon is not far from 1, this reflects a minor violation. Huynh-Feldt's has therefore be chosen for the correction. Tables of assumptions can be found in 6F.

Hypothesis one

It is predicted that participants will attribute fewer mental capacities to food animals than to companion animals.

The main effect of category showed a statistically significant differences in BAM between categories, $F(2.29, 153.66) = 63.237$, $p < .001$, partial $n^2 = .49$. To investigate where these differences lie, pairwise comparisons were examined.

Pairwise comparisons revealed significant differences between all pairs of categories except between cold blooded and pest animals.

The largest difference lay between the companion category ($M= 351.22$, $SD= 44.78$) and the cold blooded category ($M= 305.52$, $SD=59.46$), a mean difference of 46.41, $SE = 4.80$, which was significant ($p < .0005$). This is followed by the companion and pest categories ($M= 313.81$, $SD= 48.48$), with a mean difference of 37.63, $SE = 3.25$, which was significant ($p < .0005$). Third, the difference between the companion and food categories ($M=322.01$, $SD=50.45$), with a mean difference of 29.56, $SE = 2.89$, which was significant. Followed by the food and cold blooded categories, with a mean difference of 16.89, *SE* = 3.84, which was significant. The next largest mean difference (8.78, *SE* = 3.48) between cold blooded and pest, was not significant (*p* = .084). Finally, the smallest difference lay between the food and pest category, mean difference 8.11, *SE* = 2.86, which was significant (*p* = .036).

Hypothesis two

It was predicted there would be a significant association between ATA and BAM, with higher levels of ATA being associated with higher levels of BAM. A scatterplot however, revealed no linear or monotonic relationship between attitudes towards animals and BAM. No further analysis could be conducted as these assumptions for further analysis (i.e. Pearson's Correlation), were not met. Hypotheses two is therefore rejected.

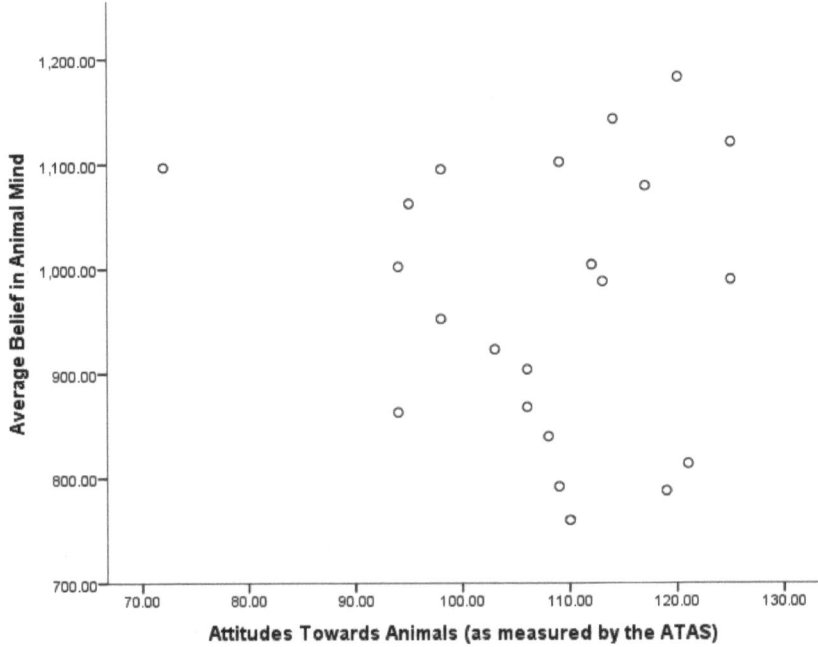

Figure 1 Scatterplot showing association between BAM and Attitudes towards Animals

Hypothesis three

It was predicted BAM would be significantly lower in the image condition than in word condition. The main effect of condition used a mixed AVONA showed no statistically significant difference in BAM between the control and image condition, $F(1,67) = 1.47$, $p = .23$, partial $n^2 = .021$. BAM however, was consistently lower in the image condition than in the control condition, as shown in the descriptive statistics table (Table 1).

Table 1 Descriptive Statistics - Mean level of BAM between conditions and categories

	Participant condition	Mean	Std. Deviation	N
Food	Word	328.54	46.12	37
	Image	314.47	54.8	32
	Total	322.01	50.45	69
Companion	Word	353.62	47.60	37
	Image	348.44	41.86	32
	Total	351.22	44.78	69
Cold	Word	317.08	54.08	37
	Image	292.16	63.37	32
	Total	305.52	59.46	69
Pest	Word	319.11	47.69	37
	Image	307.69	49.42	32
	Total	313.81	48.48	69

Hypothesis four

Is was predicted that there would be a significant interaction between category and presentation condition on BAM. A mixed ANOVA revealed no statistically significant interaction between presentation and category on BAM, $F(2.29, 153.66) = 2.65$, $p = .067$, partial $n^2 = .038$. As no interaction was found the main effect of condition and main effect of category were explored.

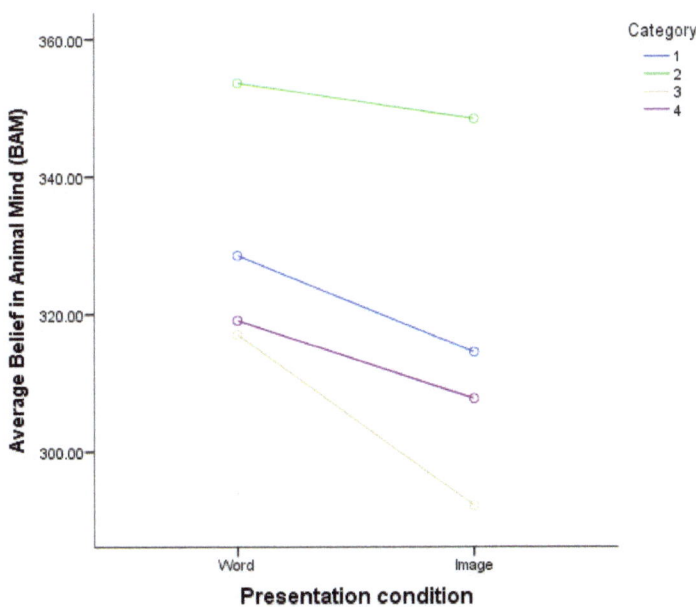

Figure 2 Graph showing the relationship between presentation condition and category on Belief in Animal Mind

Discussion

This research aimed primarily to test the effect of presentation (i.e. use of imagery) and categorisation on the attribution of mind to animals. More specifically, levels of belief in animal mind were measured across five categories of animals in one of two presentation conditions; word or image. Statistical analysis using a mixed ANOVA revealed four key findings.

The only significant relationship to be established was the effect of category on BAM. No significant interaction was found between presentation and category, as well as no significant effect of presentation on BAM, and no significant association between attitudes towards animals and BAM. Despite the rejection of most of the experimental hypotheses for the present study, this research provides a valuable extension to the current knowledge of factors influencing the attribution of mind to animals.

Category

As predicted, animal category had a significant effect on the attribution of mind, with a significant difference in BAM between food and companion groups. Consistent with the findings of Bastian et al (2012), this supports the theory that this difference in BAM allows for consumption of one and affection of the other. As Bastian's study (2012) used an exclusively psychology student sample, the current replication of findings with a predominantly non-student participant sample has increased the generalisability of these results.

The validity of this research as well as others conducted on the belief in animal mind is however limited, as cross-cultural comparisons are yet to be conducted. Despite examples of meat consumption in other cultures often being referenced in the argument for speciesism (for example the dog meat trade in Vietnam), the role of culture on the attribution of mind may be underestimated. If similar studies were conducted outside the Western culture there may be significant differences in animals categorised as food, but also differences in the relationship between BAM and animal categories (e.g. cultures that are more exposed to open animal slaughter may not experience cognitive dissonance and therefore have no need to reduce the capacity for mind of food animals).

Although the difference in BAM between food and non-food animals has been used to support the cognitive dissonance explanation of the meat paradox, it is unknown if participants actual experienced feelings of dissonance that led to the dementalisation of animals in the food category. The study conducted by Bastian (2012) attempted to create cognitive dissonance by reminding participants of a food animal's role within the meat industry. This was required in order to examine the denial of mind to food animals as a mechanism for reducing the conflict of cognitions. This present study however did not attempt to provoke feelings of dissonance, so the difference in BAM between companion and farm animals cannot be attributed to the denial of mind associated with dissonance reduction.

The present study has extended upon previous research by also examining the BAM in a range of animal categories. Results revealed a significant difference in BAM between most of the animal categories, excluding cold-blooded and pest animals. This supports the theory that the category of an animal may determine BAM, but may now be extended to include more categories, rather than simply companions and food animals.

Furthermore, the finding that BAM differed between all categories, not just between food and companion animals, suggests that there are other factors influencing BAM, rather than if the animal is categorised as food. It can be speculated that categories of animals may be attributed mind based on their usefulness. Epley, Waytz, Akalis and Cacioppo (2008) suggested that animals are attributed mind when it suits an individual's own interests.

A comparison of these categories showed that companion animals were attributed the highest level of mind, followed by food animals, cold-blooded animals and pest animals. When the theory of cognitive dissonance is applied to all of the categories it can be speculated that they are all associated with conflicting cognitions. For example, pest animals such as seagulls and foxes are frequency persecuted and face limited legal protection compared to other wild animals. When asked to consider the mental capacities of these animals, feelings of guilt may have been created. This could result in the need for a method of reducing the conflict between animals taking the form of the denial of mind.

The conclusion that pest and coldblooded animals, as well as those used for food, are attributed significantly less mind than companions may have a wide range of implications outside of the meat industry.

ATAS

Despite the previous findings of Knight et al (2004), a scatterplot (figure 1) displayed no significant correlation between scores on the ATAS and BAM. A possible explanation for this inconsistency may be use of a different tool for measuring ATA. While Knight et al (2004) measured attitudes using questions based on agreement/disagreement with various animal uses (e.g. the use of animals for entertainment), the present study used a questionnaire designed to measure attitudes of sensitivity towards the maltreatment of animals.

This contrast of results between studies suggests that the ATAS may measure something different to that measured by Knight et al (2004) (find name of measure). It could be argued that ATA may be too complex to measured using Likert style responses in questionnaires. As pointed out by Henry (2004), it is unclear what exactly is being measured by the ATAS. As this scale includes a number of questions that refer to categories of animals (e.g. food, pets), others are more vague. Combined with the findings of the present study showing a significant relationship between category and BAM, the ATAS may not have provided an accurate representation of ATA, as the final score fails to account for any differences between categories.

In conclusion, the findings of the present study in combination with previous research suggests the need for a more reliable and representative measure of attitudes towards animals which controls for the effect of categorisation on the perception of animals.

Presentation

The finding that presentation had no significant effect on BAM of food animals means the hypothesis that food animals would be attributed higher mind in the image condition than control condition can be rejected.

The hypothesis that the use of imagery would have a significant effect on BAM was based on the research of Monteiro (2012) which, unlike the present study, used images of animals clearly shown as property of the farming industry of varying degrees of graphic detail. This approach was not replicated in the present study not only for ethical reasons, but also because the low detail image was found to have the greatest effect on attitudes towards animal rights. It may be that no significant relationship was found between presentation (word/image) and BAM because the images of food animals used contained no indicators of the animal's connection to the food industry.

Similarly to ATA, it is difficult to draw conclusions from this research in terms of cognitive dissonance. This is because neither can be physically observed and thus cannot be objectively measured. For example, cognitive dissonance could be used as an explanation for why the high graphic images in the Monetiro study had the smallest effect on ATA (as the images would cause feelings of dissonance which could be reduced by decreasing the animals' capacity for mind). However there is objective way to determine the level of dissonance experienced by participants in order to compare between the high and low graphic images groups.

The use of imagery as a variable, however, on the attribution of mind should not be dismissed. Despite the analysis showing no significant differences in animal mind between presentation conditions, descriptive statistics (Table 1) showed BAM to be consistently lower in the image condition than in the word condition.

It is possible that with a larger sample the effect of imagery of BAM may be significant. While the current sample may be more representative than a solely student sample of participants, there are still limits to data collected. The simple demographics for participants did not match between the independent conditions, which may have had a significant effect on the results. The main difference between conditions was the method of recruitment, which in turn influenced other participant variables such as age, level of education and geographical location (i.e. UK, America). The control group was mainly comprised of participants recruited using Hanover, including no students, while the experimental condition included a combination of both. Those recruiting using Hanover were often not current students, American, and older than student participants in the experimental condition. With a small sample, as with this research, differences between participants such as these can have a confounding effect on the results.

The present study has demonstrated the powerful influence of animal category on the mind that appears to be consistent both within student and general population participant samples. While this finding has yet be replicated outside of Western cultures it may help increase the understanding of the vast difference in the treatment of animals across the world. Although the effect of imagery on BAM was shown not to be significant, the consistent difference between conditions suggests the need for further exploration of this variable.

It can be concluded that future research examine the relationship between imagery and BAM, whilst control the effect of category using a greater variation of imagery. A wide range of participants should be recruited rather than focusing on student, but also to match participants between conditions as closely as possible. This is important as the interaction between presentation and category on BAM may be discrete, therefore confounding variables must be controlled.

References

Aronson, E. (1968). Dissonance theory: Progress and problems. In R. P. Abelson, E. Aronson, W. J. McGuire, T. M. Newcomb, M. J. Rosenberg, & P. H. Tannenbaum, *Theories of cognitive consistency: A sourcebook* (pp. 5-27). Chicago: Rand McNally.

Aronson, E. (1999). Dissonance, hypocrisy, and the self-concept. In E. Harmon-Jones, & J. Mills, *Cognitive dissonance: Progress on a pivotal theory in social psychology* (pp. 103-126). Washington, DC: American Psychological Association.

Aronson, E., & Mills, J. (1959). The effect of severity of initiation on liking for a group. *Journal of Abnormal and Social Psychology, 59*, 177-181.

B, H. (n.d.). The Relationship between Animal Cruelty, Delinquency, and Attidues toward the Treatment of Animals.

Bandura, A. (1991). Moral disengagement in the perpetration of inhumanities. *Personality and Social Psychology Review, 3*, 193-209.

Bandura, A., Barbaranelli, C., Caprara, G. V., & Pastorelli, C. (1996). Mechanisms of moral disengagement in the exercise of moral agency. *Journal of Personality and Social Psychology, 71*, 364-374.

Bastian, B. L. (2012). Don't Mind Meat? The Denial of Mind to Animals Used for Human Consumption. *Personality and Social Psychology Bulletin*, 247-256.

Bem, D. J. (1972). Self-perception theory. In L. Berkowitz, *Advances in experimental social psychology* (Vol. 6, pp. 1-62). New York: Academic Press.

Bratanova, B., Loughnan, S., & Bastian, B. (2011). The effect of categorization as food on the perceived moral standing of animals. *Appetite*, 193-196.

Brehm, J. W. (1956). Postdecision changes in the desirability of alternatives. *Journal of Abnormal and Social Psychology, 52*, 384-389.

Castono, E., & Giner-Sorolla, R. (2006). Not quite human: Infra-humanisation in response to collective responsibility for inter-group killing. *Journal of Personality and Social Psychology, 90*, 804-818.

Chaiken, S., & Baldwin, M. (1981). Affective-Cognitive Consistency and the Effect of Salient Behavioural Information on the Self Perception of Attitudes. *Journal of Personality and Social Psychology, 41*, 1-19.

Cooper, J., & Fazio, R. H. (1984). A new look at dissonance theory. Orlando, FL: Academic Press.

Cuddy, A. J., Rock, M. S., & Norton, M. I. (2007). Aid in the aftermath of Hurrican Katrina: Inferences of secondary emotions and intergroup helping behaviour. *Group Processes & Intergroup Relations, 10*, 107-118.

Darwin, C. (1871). *The Descent of Man and Selection in Relation to Sex.* London: J Murray.

Davis, M. H. (1980). A multidimensional approach to individual differences in empathy. *Catalog of Selected Documents in Psychology, 10*(85).

Department for Environmental, F. a. (2014, December 11). *GOV.CO.UK.* Retrieved from https://www.gov.uk/government/statistics/family-food-2013

Discoll, J. W. (1992). Attitudes toward animal use. *Anthrozoos, 5*, 32-39.

Eddy, T. J., Gallup, G. G., & Povinelli, D. J. (n.d.). Attribution of cognitive states to animals: Anthropomorphism in comparative perspective. *Journal of Social Issues, 49*, 87-101.

Epley, N., Waytz, A., Akalis, S., & Cacioppo, J. T. (2008). When we need a human: Motivational determinants of anthromorphism. *Social Cognition, 26*, 143-155.

Festinger, L. (1957). *A theory of cognitive dissonance.* Stanford, CA: Stanford University Press.

Festinger, L., & Carlsmith, J. M. (1959). Cognitive consequences of forced compliance. *Journal of Abnormal and Social Psychology, 58*, 203-210.

Festinger, L., Riecken, H. W., & Schachter, S. (1956). *When Prophecy Fails: A Social and Psychological Study of a Modern Group that Predicted the Destruction of the World.* University of Minnesota Press.

Food Safety Authority of Ireland. (2013, January 15). FSAI Survey Finds Horse DNA in Some Beef Burder Products. Retrieved from https://www.fsai.ie/news_centre/press_releases/horseDNA15012013.html

Furnham, A., McManus, C., & Scott, D. (2003). Personality, empathy and attitudes towards animal welfare. *Anthrozoos, 16*, 135-146.

Gallup, G. G., Jr, & Beckstead, J. W. (1988). Attitudes toward animal research. *American Psychologist, 43*, 474-476.

Grey, H. M., Grey, K., & Wegner, D. M. (2007). Dimensions of mind perception. *Science, 315*, 619-621.

Harmon-Jones, E., & Mills, J. (1999). *Cognitive Dissonance: Perspectives on a pivotal theory in social psychology.* Washington, DC: American Psychological Association.

Henry, B. C. (2004). The relationship between animal cruelty, delinquency, and attitudes toward the treatment of animals. *Society and Animals.*

Herzog, H. (2010). *Some we love, some we hate, some we eat: Why it's so hard to think straight about animals.* New York: Harper Collins.

Herzog, H. A., Betchart, .. S., & Pittman, R. B. (1991). Gender, sex role orientation and attitudes toward animals. *Anthrozoos, 4*, 184-191.

Hutchins, M. E., & Armstrong, J. B. (1994). College students attitudes toward animal use. *College Student Journal, 28*, 258-266.

Kimbal, R., & Broida, J. P. (1991). Psychological profiles of students for and against vivisection using the Myers-Briggs Type Indicator. *Humane Innovations and Alternatives, 5*, 232-235.

Knight, S., Vrij, A., Cherryman, J., & Nunkoosing, K. (2004). Attitudes towards animal use and belief in animal mind. *Anthrozoos, 17*, 43.

Kozak, M., Marsh, A., & Wegner, D. (2006). What do I think you're doing? Action identification and mind attribution. *Journal of Personality and Social Psychology, 90*, 543-555.

Kozak, M., Marsh, A., & Wegner, D. (2006). What do I think you're doing? Action identification and mind attribution. *Journal of Personality and Social Psychology, 90,* 543-555.

Laham, S. (2009). Expanding the moral circle: Inclusion and exclusion mindsets and the circle of moral regard. *Journal of Experimental Social Psychology, 45,* 250-253.

Loughman, S., & Bastian, B. (2011). Perceptions of meat animals by Vegetarians and Non-Vegetarians. University of Melbourne, Unpublished Work.

Loughnan, S., Haslam, N., & Bastian, B. (2010). The role of meat consumption in the denial of mind and moral status in animals. *Appetite, 55,* 156-159.

Low, P., Panksepp, J., Reiss, D., Edelman, D., Van Swinderen, B., & Koch, C. (2012). The Cambridge Declaration on Consciousness. *Francis Crick Memorial Conference on Consciousness in Human and non-Human Animals.* Cambridge. Retrieved from http://fcmconference.org

Monterio, C. (2012, October 17). *One Perspective on the Effects of Graphic Images on Attitudes towards Animal Rights.* Retrieved from FARM: http://blog.farmusa.org/the-effects-of-graphic-images-on-attitudes-towards-animal-rights/

Morewedge, C., K., Preston, J., & Wegner, D. M. (2007). Timescale bias in the attribution of mind. *Journal of Personality and Social Psychology, 93,* 1-11.

Morris, M. (2014, January 14). Horsemeat scandal: How tastes changed. BBC. Retrieved from http://www.bbc.co.uk/news/business-25715666

Persaud, R. (2013, April 22). The Horse Meat Scandals Reveal We Are More Psychologically Screwed Up Than We Realised About Eating Animals. Retrieved from http://www.huffingtonpost.co.uk/dr-raj-persaud/horse-meat-scandal-eating-meat_b_2720783.html

Regan, T. (1997). The rights of humans and other animals. *Ethics and Behaviour, 7,* 103-111.

Richardson, N. J. (1994b). Meat consumption, definition of meat and trust in information sources in the UK population and members of The Vegetarian Society. *Ecology of Food and Nutrition*.

Safeway. (1991). Today's vegetarian shopper: a survey by Safeway into the reactions of vegetarians. *Home Economist*(6), 17-18.

Singer. (1990). *Animal liberation.* New York: Random House.

Steele, C. M. (1988). The psychology of self-affirmation: Sustaining the integrity of the self. In L. Berkowitz, *Advances in experimental social psychology* (Vol. 21, pp. 261-302). San Diego, CA: Academic Press.

Stibbe, A. (2001). Language, power and the social construction of animals. *Soc. Anim.*, 145-161.

Wilson, T., & Hodges, S. (1992). Attitudes as temporary constructions. In L. Martin, & A. Tesser, *The construction of social judgement* (pp. 37-65). Hillsdale, NJ: Erlbaum.

Woodward, J. (1988). Comsumer attitudes towards meat and meat products. *British Food Journal*(90), 101-104.

Wuensch, K. L., Jenkins, K. W., & Poteat, G. (2002). Misanthropy, idealism, and attitudes towards animals. *Anthrozoos, 15*, 139-149.

Appendix 1A
Demographic questionnaire

The following questionnaire is designed to collect your basic information and should take no longer than ten minutes. Selected you responses from the options provided or write in the text box where appropriate. Please take your time to answer questions carefully. Remember you have the right to withdraw at any time.

1. **Are you?**
   - Male
   - Female
2. **Year of birth?**
3. **Are you a student at the University of Worcester?**
   - Yes
   - No
4. **Type of study**
   - Student only
   - Student and part-time work
   - Student and volunteer work
   - N/A
5. **Are you studying a…?**
   - Single honours degree
   - Dual honours degree
   - Other
   - N/A
6. **What subject/s are you studying? (if applicable)**
7. **What is your ethnicity? (Please select all that apply)**
   - American Indian or Alaskan Native
   - Asian or Pacific Islander
   - Black or African American
   - Hispanic or Latino
   - White / Caucasian
   - Prefer not to answer
   - Other (please specify)

8. **Do you identify with any of the following religions? (Please select all that apply)**
- Protestantism
- Catholicism
- Christianity
- Judaism
- Islam
- Buddhism
- Hinduism
- Native American
- Inter/Non-denominational
- No religion
- Other (please specify)

9. **Do you identify with any of the following political parties?**
- Liberal Democrats
- Conservative
- Labour
- United Kingdom Independence Party (UKIP)
- No interest in politics
- Other (please specify)

10. **Are you…?**
- Vegan
- Vegetarian
- Neither

11. In the last four weeks, how often have you eaten the following?

	Once a day or day	Once or more a week	Once or more a month	Less than once a month	Never	N/A
Beef						
Mutton						
Chicken						
Pork						
Lamb						
Duck						

12. What are the main influences on your diet? (Place in rank order, with 1 having the greatest influence and 5 have the least influence)
- Health
- Weight (e.g. loss/gain)
- Price
- Ethical considerations (e.g. fair-trade, free-range)
- Convenience

13. Do you, or have you, owned any of the following?
- Dog
- Cat
- Rabbit
- Hamster
- Parrot
- Horse
- Other (please specify)

14. **How would you rate your level of attachment to your pets?**
    - Very weak
    - Weak
    - Mediocre
    - Strong
    - Very strong
15. **How would you rate your level of consideration towards animals in everyday choices?**

1	2	3	4	5
I never consider animals		I sometimes consider animals		I always consider animals

Appendix 2B

Attitudes towards the Treatment of Animals Scale (Henry, 2004)

The following questionnaire is designed to investigate your attitudes towards the treatment of various animals. Your answers answer will be recorded on a scale between 1 and 5.

1	2	3	4	5
Not at all				A lot

Lower answers correspond to a lower level of concern, and high answers represent a higher level of concern in response to the question.

1. How much would it bother you to think about someone intentionally killing a domestic stock animal (horse, cow, pig) other than for food or to help the animal because the animal was hurt, old, or sick?
2. How much would it bother you to think about someone intentionally killing a wild animal (deer, rabbit, squirrel) other than for food, while hunting, or to help the animal because the animal was hurt or sick?
3. How much would it bother you to think about someone intentionally killing a companion animal (pet dog, cat, rabbit) other than to help the animal because the animal was hurt, old or sick?
4. How much would it bother you to think about someone intentionally killing a domestic stock animal or wild animal for food?
5. How much would it bother you to think about someone intentionally killing a wild animal while hunting?
6. How much would it bother you to think about someone intentionally killing an animal because the animal was hurt, old, or sick (euthanasia)?
7. How much would it bother you to think about someone intentionally killing (euthanising) a companion animal or domestic animal because the owner is unable to care for the animal (the person is moving out of state and cannot take the animal to the new home)?
8. How much would it bother you to think about someone intentionally hurting a domestic stock animal (horse, cow, pig) other than for training, branding?

9. How much wold it bother you to think about someone intentionally hurting a wild animal (deer, rabbit, squirrel)?
10. How much would it bother you to think about someone intentionally hurting a companion animal (pet dog, cat, rabbit) other than for training?
11. How much would it bother you to think about someone having sexual contact with an animal?
12. How much would it bother you to think about someone using mice/birds/reptiles in research that results in serious injury, illness, or death of the animal?
13. How much would it bother you to think about someone using mice/birds/reptiles in research that does NOT result in serious injury, illness, or death of the animal?
14. How much would it bother you to think about someone using dogs or cats in research that results in serious injury, illness, or death of the animal?
15. How much would it bother you to think about someone using dogs or cats in research that does NOT result in serious injury, illness, or death of the animal?
16. How much would it bother you to think about someone using primates (monkeys, chimpanzees) in research that results in serious injury, illness, or death of the animal?
17. How much would it bother you to think about someone using primates (monkeys, chimpanzees) in research that does NOT result in serious injury, illness, or death of the animal?
18. How much would it bother you to think about someone failing to provide medical care for a domestic stock animal who is clearly injured or ill?
19. How much would it bother you to think about someone failing to provide medical care for a companion animal who is clearly injured or ill?
20. How much would it bother you to think about someone failing to provide domestic stock animals or companion animals with food or water for 24 hours?
21. How much would it bother you to think about someone leaving domestic stock animals outside without shelter for 24 hours?
22. How much would it bother you to think about someone leaving companion animals outside without shelter for 24 hours?

23. How much would it bother you to think about someone leaving a companion animal in a locked car with the windows cracked with an outside temperature of 70° for one hour?
24. How much would it bother you to think about someone intentionally hurting a domestic stock animal for the purposes of training the animal (hitting the animal to encourage it to behave in a particular manner)?
25. How much would it bother you to think about someone intentionally hurting a companion animal for the purposes of training the animal (using a shock collar to train a dog)?
26. How much would it bother you to think about someone intentionally encouraging or causing animals to fight one another (dog fighting, cock fighting, etc.)?

Appendix 3C

Mental Capacity Rating Task

Control (word) condition

- Food group; Cow, chicken, duck, lamb, sheep, pig.
- Companion group; Cat, dog, hamster, horse, rabbit, parrot.
- Wild mammal group; Bear, dolphin, elephant, gorilla, lion, buffalo.
- Wild reptile/amphibian group; crocodile, frog, komodo-dragon, lizard, tortoise, snake.
- Pest group; Badger, pigeon, rat, slug, seagull, fox.

Image condition

Food group;

Companion group;

Wild mammal group;

Wild cold-blooded group;

Pest animals;

Appendix 4D

Participant Information Sheet

Title of Project

An investigation into the relationship between moral consideration and the sentience of animals

Invitation

We would like to invite you to take part in a research project. Before you decide whether to take part it is important that you understand why the research is being done and what it will involve. Please take time to read this carefully and ask the researcher if you have any questions. Talk to others about the study if you wish. You will have at least two days to decide if you want to take part.

What is the purpose of the study?

This study aims to examine the relationship between the perceptions of animals and the moral consideration they receive.

Why have I been invited to take part?

You have received this invitation because you are an undergraduate psychology student at the University of Worcester. We are hoping to recruit a total of 80 participants for this study.

Do I have to take part?

No. It is up to you to decide whether or not you want to take part in this study. If you do decide to take part you will be asked to sign a consent form.

What will happen to me if I agree to take part?

If you agree to take part you will;

- Be asked to read a sign a consent form stating that your participant in this research is voluntary and that you understand your rights as a participant.
- Be required to take part in the separate components of the study.
    - Part 1, demographic information questionnaire – 10 minutes
    - Part 2, attitudes towards animals scale – 15 minutes

- o Part 3, animal sentience flashcard experiment – 20 minutes
    - You will be required to rate the mental capacities (such as pleasure, hunger) possessed by a range of different animals, as well a self-rated score for both the moral consideration you believe the animal deserves and how you would feel about eating the animal.
- This study will be conducted online using the questionnaire-building tool 'SurveyMonkey', which is accessible anywhere using your University of Worcester student account.
- This study will take approximately 35 minutes to complete
- The data will be automatically recorded using SurveyMonkey

Are there any disadvantages risks to taking part?

There are no obvious risks to taking part in this research. However, this research has been ethically approved and follows strict ethical guidelines. In the event that you feel uncomfortable with the research or have any complaints, contact details for relevant persons can be found at the end of this document.

Will the information I give stay confidential?

Everything you say/report is confidential unless you tell us something that indicates that you or someone else is at risk of harm. We would discuss this with you before telling anyone else. The information you give may be used for a research report, but it will not be possible to identify you from our research report or any other dissemination activities. Your original data will be securely stored and kept until project ends in December and then securely disposed of. The analysis of data (e.g. statistics) will be securely stored and may be used for further research purposes.

What will happen to the results of the research study?

This research is being carried out as part of my undergraduate degree at the University of Worcester. The findings of this study will be reported as part of my dissertation and may also be published in academic journals or at conferences.

If you wish to receive a summary of the research findings please contact the researcher.

Who is organising the research?

This research has been approved by the University Of Worcester Institute Of Health Ethics Committee.

What happens next?

Please keep this information sheet. If you do decide to take part, please continue to the next page.

Thank you for taking the time to read this information

If you decide to take part of you have any questions, concerns or complaints about this study please contact one of the research team using the details below.

Student researcher	Supervisor
Emmeline Cambridge	Dr Helen Scott
XXXXX@XXXXX.uk	XXXXX@XXXXX.uk

If you would like to speak to an independent person who is not a member of the research team, please contact John-Paul Wilson at the University of Worcester, using the following details:

John-Paul Wilson
Research Manager
Graduate Research School
University of Worcester
Henwick Grove
Worcester WR2 6AJ
01905 542196
XXXXX@XXXXX.uk

Appendix 5E
Participant Consent Form

Title of project

An investigation into the relationship between attitudes towards animals and perceived level of mental capacity.

Name of Researcher

Emmeline Cambridge

Please read and evaluate the following statements. This is to provide your consent to taking part in this study.

- I confirm that I have read and understood the information sheet for the above study and have had the opportunity to ask questions.

    Agree ☐   Disagree ☐

- I confirm that I have had sufficient time to consider whether I want to take part in this study.

    Agree ☐   Disagree ☐

- I understand that I do not have to take part in this research and I can change my mind at any time.

    Agree ☐   Disagree ☐

- I agree to my research data (including quotations) being used in publications or reports.

    Agree ☐   Disagree ☐

- I agree to take part in this study.

    Agree ☐   Disagree ☐

- I have been made aware of support services that are available.

    Agree ☐   Disagree ☐

- I know who to contact if I have any concerns about this research.

    Agree ☐   Disagree ☐

Appendix 6F

Analysis output

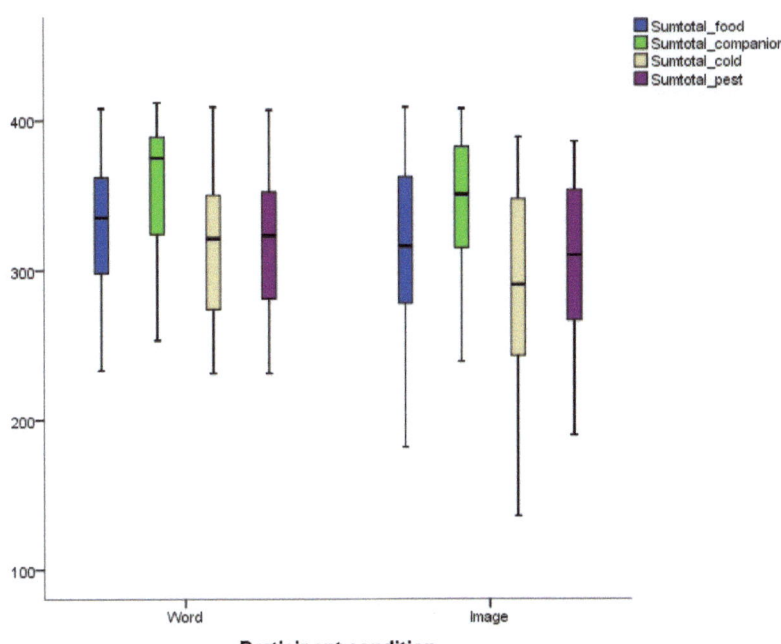

Figure 3 Boxplot for outliers

	Participant condition	Shapiro-Wilk Statistic	df	Sig.
Food	Word	.97	37	.31
	Image	.96	32	.28
Companion	Word	.89	37	.001
	Image	.96	32	.20
Mammal	Word	.87	37	.000
	Image	.97	32	.564
Cold	Word	.95	37	.085
	Image	.97	32	.39
Pest	Word	.97	37	.52
	Image	.96	32	.35

Table 2 Levene's Test of Equality of Error Variances

	F	df1	df2	Sig.
Food	.937	1	67	.337
Companion	.798	1	67	.375
Mammal	7.881	1	67	.007
Cold	.594	1	67	.443
Pest	.025	1	67	.874

Table 3 Box's Test of Equality of Covariance Matrices

Box's M	22.329
F	2.087
df1	10
df2	20,423.381
Sig.	.022

Table 4 Mauchly's Test of Sphericity

Mauchly's Test of Sphericity							
					Epsilon[b]		
Within Subjects Effect	Mauchly's W	Approx. Chi-Square	df	Sig.	Greenhouse-Geisser	Huynh-Feldt	Lower-bound
Category	.598	33.777	5	.000	.728	.764	.333

Table 5 Mixed ANOVA testing for the effect of category, and the interaction between category and condition on BAM

Source		df	Mean Square	F	Sig.	Partial Eta Squared
Category	Sphericity Assumed	3	27854.151	63.237	.000	.486
	Huynh-Feldt	2.293	36435.246	63.237	.000	.486
	Lower-bound	1.000	83562.454	63.237	.000	.486
Category * Condition	Sphericity Assumed	3	1165.069	2.645	.050	.038
	Huynh-Feldt	2.293	1523.995	2.645	.067	.038
Error(Category)	Sphericity Assumed	201	440.473			
	Huynh-Feldt	153.661	576.170			

Table 6 Pairwise comparisons between categories measuring BAM

(I) Category	(J) Category	Mean Difference (I-J)	Std. Error	Sig.
Food	Companion	-29.53*	2.891	<.001
	Cold	16.89*	3.842	<.00
	Pest	8.107*	2.861	.036
Companion	Cold	46.11	4.80	.000
	Pest	37.63*	3.25	.000
Cold	Pest	-8.78	3.47	.084